THIS BOOK BELONGS TO:

____

ISBN: 9798716748460

FIRST EDITION

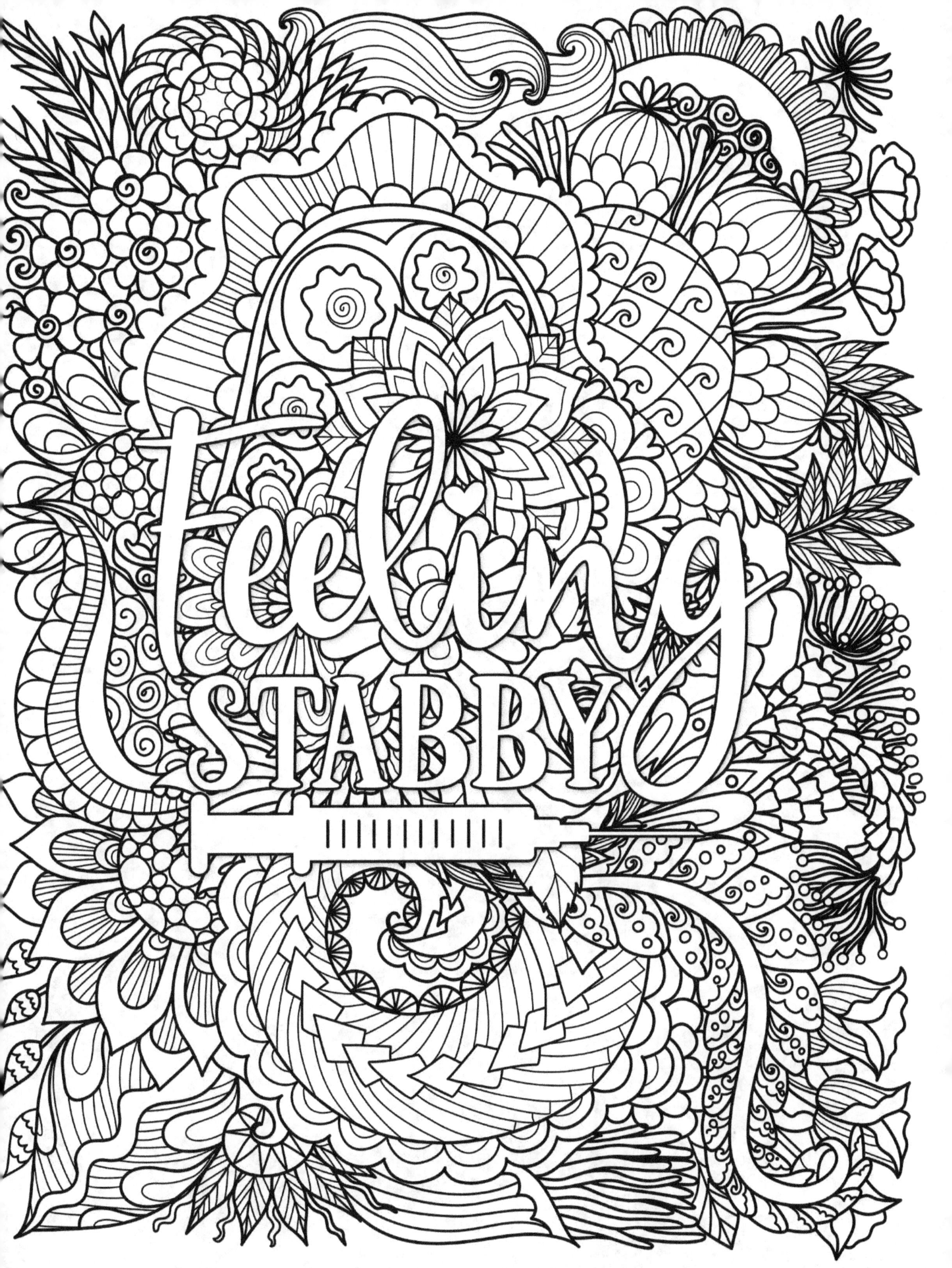
feeling
STABBY

WILL TRADE
MEDICAL
ADVICE FOR
WINE

Coffee
SCRUBS
& RUBBER
gloves

SUPER
nurse

EDUCATED
DRUG
dealer

Chaos
COORDINATOR
#NURSELIFE

scrubs on
bun hair
up all night
don't care
#nurselife

Be Safe
Drink With
A NURSE

SLEEP
all day
NURSE
ALL NIGHT

THE VEIN
whisperer

slingin
PILLS
to pay the
BILLS
Rx

THIS SUPERHERO
WEARS
SCRUBS

RESTING
nurse
FACE

nursing
IS A WORK
of heart

nurses
NEED
shots too

nurses
Do It
BETTER

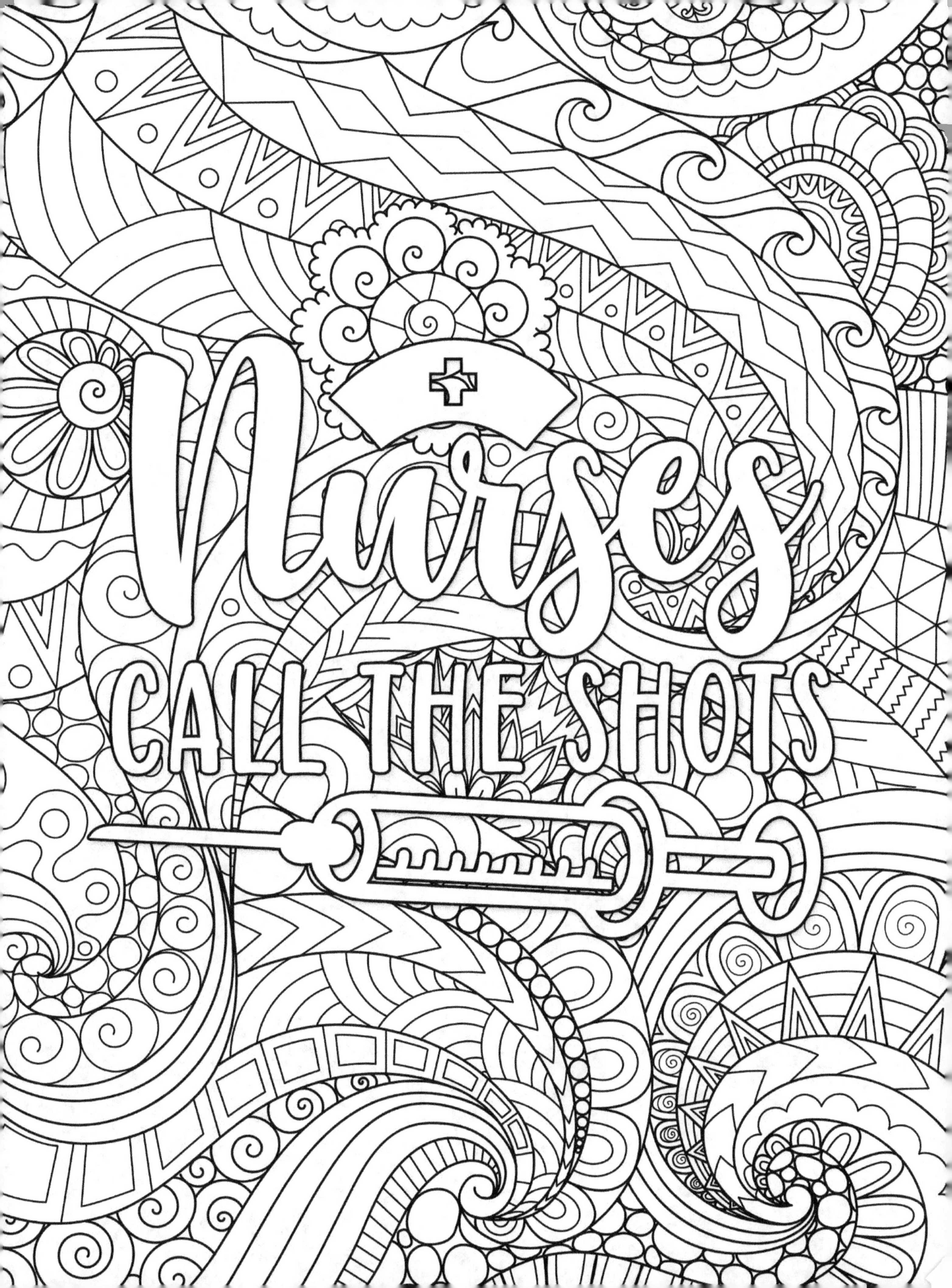
Nurses
CALL THE SHOTS

nurse
SQUAD

NOT ALL angels HAVE WINGS SOME HAVE stethoscopes

NACHO
average
NURSE

My Blood
Type
Is
Coffee

NURSES
we can't fix
STUPID
but we can
SEDATE IT

living that
NURSE
life

I'M A
nurse
WHAT'S YOUR
super power?

FIRST I DRINK
The coffee
THEN I SAVE
The lives

DON'T FLATTER
Yourself
I WAS LOOKING
AT YOUR VEINS

NURSE SURVIVAL
CAFFEINE
before shift
ALCOHOL
after shift

Don't mess
WITH ME
I get paid
TO STAB PEOPLE

A good vein
is what dreams
are made of
#nurselife

CUTE ENOUGH TO
Stop your heart
SKILLED ENOUGH TO
Restart it

www.ingramcontent.com/pod-product-compliance
Lightning Source LLC
Chambersburg PA
CBHW081538220526
45467CB00010B/3243
9798716748460